You and the Law

Jennifer Overend Prior, Ph.D.

Consultants

Shelley Scudder
Gifted Education Teacher
Broward County Schools

Caryn Williams, M.S.Ed.
Madison County Schools
Huntsville, AL

Publishing Credits

Conni Medina, M.A.Ed., *Managing Editor*
Lee Aucoin, *Creative Director*
Torrey Maloof, *Editor*
Marissa Rodriguez, *Designer*
Stephanie Reid, *Photo Editor*
Rachelle Cracchiolo, M.S.Ed., *Publisher*

Image Credits: pp. 6, 14 Alamy; pp. 25 pp. 26–27 Associated Press; p. 12 FDA photo by Michael J. Ermarth; pp. 4, 13, 18, 20, 21, 22 Getty Images; p. 27 imagebroker/Jim West/Newscom; p. 10 iStockphoto; p. 29 Joey Rice; pp. 14–15 ClassicStock/Alamy, 1819 (Public Domain) via WIkimedia; p. 17 The Library of Congress [LC-USZ62-75334]; p. 19 National Archives; p. 16 Science Source; pp. 11, 32 ThinkStock; All other images from Shutterstock.

Teacher Created Materials
5301 Oceanus Drive
Huntington Beach, CA 92649-1030
http://www.tcmpub.com

ISBN 978-1-4333-6994-0

Table of Contents

Students say the Pledge of Allegiance.

Justice for All

At school, have you ever said the Pledge of Allegiance (uh-LEE-juhns)? The last line says, “With liberty and justice for all.” This means we should all be free to live as we want. And it means everyone deserves a fair chance to **succeed** (suhk-SEED).

Liberty and Justice For All

Liberty means that people are able to act and speak freely. *Justice* means to be fair. It means to use laws to decide if someone's actions are good or bad. All American **citizens** (SIT-uh-zuhns) deserve liberty and justice.

The Pledge of Allegiance

I pledge allegiance
to the Flag
of the United States of America,
and to the Republic
for which it stands,
one Nation
under God,
indivisible,
with liberty and justice for all.

The United States thinks all people should be free and safe. **Laws** protect our liberty and justice. Laws help make our country great.

Our Laws

We all follow rules. A rule at home may tell you to walk indoors. Rules at school remind you to be kind. Rules keep us safe and happy.

These are rules for a classroom.

A law is a type of rule people must follow. Without laws, there would be no order. Laws protect us. They help us make good choices.

The law says you have to wear a helmet when riding a bicycle.

Local Laws

Local laws help people live together. A local law may tell stores to use paper bags instead of plastic bags. Or a law may say where a house can be built.

This woman's local store uses paper bags. It is the law in her city.

Local laws help people who live together in communities (kuh-MYOO-ni-teez) get along. They tell neighbors to be quiet late at night. They tell people where they can park their cars. Different cities can have different laws.

In this city, it is against the law to park on this part of the street.

State Laws

Communities have local laws. State laws are about bigger issues. Everyone in the state must follow state laws.

This woman is making sure workers are paid the right amount.

State laws tell businesses how much they must pay workers. There are also state laws about how to drive cars. Each state has its own set of laws.

This girl follows the law by riding in a car seat.

National Laws

In 1787, the United States formed a nation. The states decided to share many laws. Everyone in the country must follow these **national** laws.

Another Way

Some children go to school at home. These students learn the same things that students in schools learn. They just do it in a different place.

These kids are homeschooled.

National laws say who can be an American citizen. There are laws that say all children must go to school. Some laws keep our food safe. Other laws tell people how to build roads and highways.

The two men on the left are checking to make sure our food is safe to eat.

The Constitution

The **government** (GUHV-ern-muhnt) makes the laws for our country. Some laws have been around for a long time. Thousands of new laws are passed every year.

This is the Constitution.

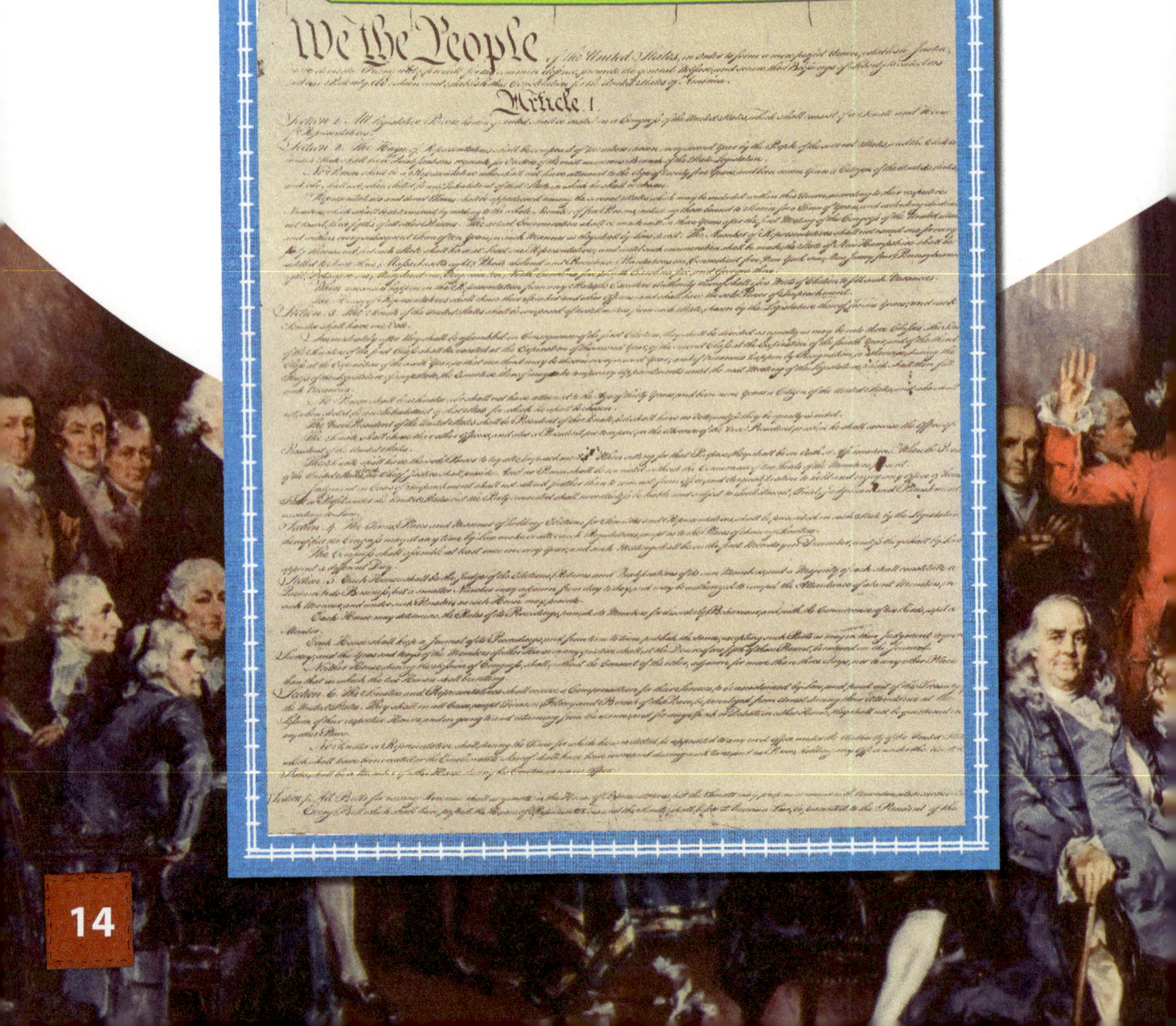

The Constitution (kon-sti-TOO-shuhn) is the main set of laws for our country. It says how our country works and should run. The Constitution was written in 1787.

America's leaders write the Constitution.

This is the Bill of Rights.

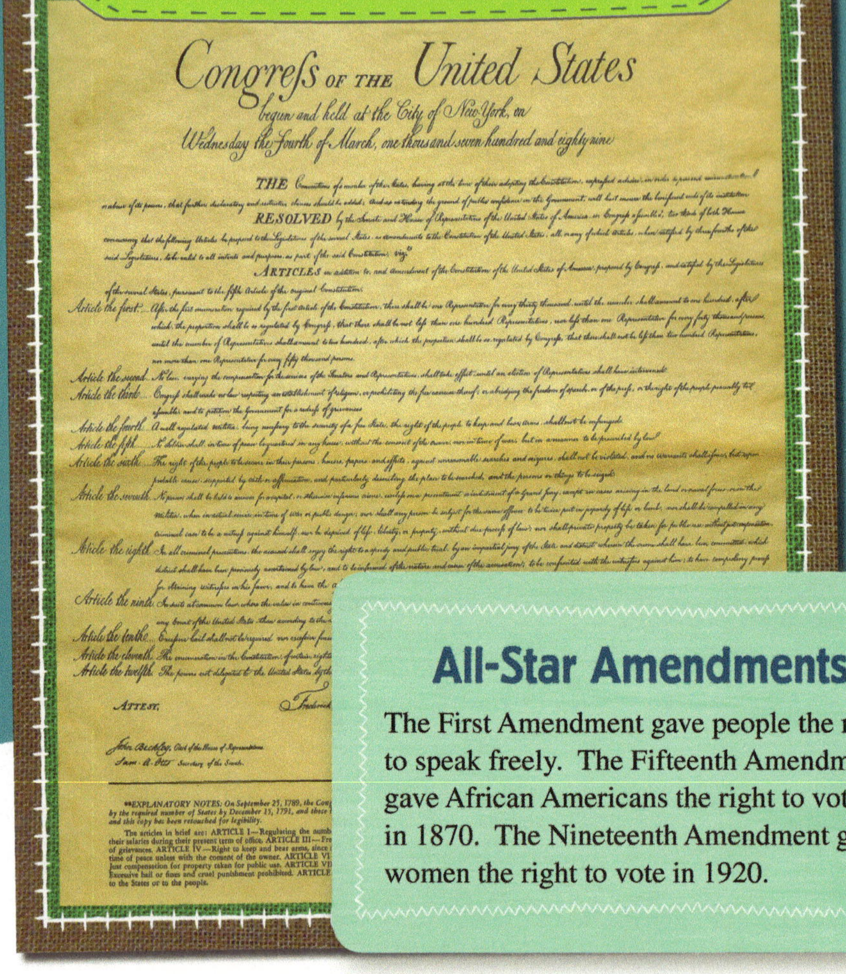
Congrefs of the United States
begun and held at the City of New-York, on
Wednesday the Fourth of March, one thousand seven hundred and eighty nine

All-Star Amendments

The First Amendment gave people the right to speak freely. The Fifteenth Amendment gave African Americans the right to vote in 1870. The Nineteenth Amendment gave women the right to vote in 1920.

Changing a Law

The government can change the Constitution by adding **amendments** (uh-MEND-muhnts). Amendments are changes for the better. We have added 27 amendments to the Constitution.

These women are voting for the first time.

The first ten amendments are known as the Bill of Rights. Every citizen has these ten rights. The Bill of Rights says that the government will not take away these rights.

Making a Law

The Constitution is important. But sometimes, new laws are needed. A law begins as an idea. An idea for a law is called a *bill*. Anyone with an idea can write a bill. Even you!

This bill was made a law in 1941. It helped keep America safe during World War II.

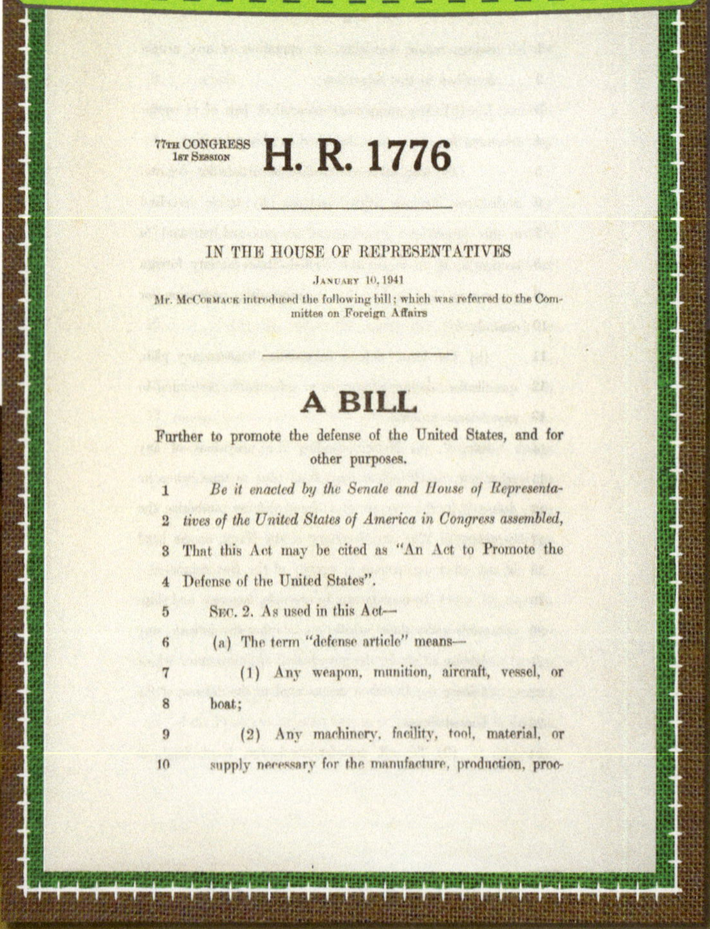

77th CONGRESS
1st Session
H. R. 1776

IN THE HOUSE OF REPRESENTATIVES

January 10, 1941

Mr. McCormack introduced the following bill; which was referred to the Committee on Foreign Affairs

A BILL

Further to promote the defense of the United States, and for other purposes.

Be it enacted by the Senate and House of Representatives of the United States of America in Congress assembled, That this Act may be cited as "An Act to Promote the Defense of the United States".

Sec. 2. As used in this Act—

(a) The term "defense article" means—

(1) Any weapon, munition, aircraft, vessel, or boat;

(2) Any machinery, facility, tool, material, or supply necessary for the manufacture, production, proc-

People can send their ideas for new bills to **Congress** (KONG-gris). Congress is the group that makes laws for our country.

These are members of Congress.

Who Has the Vote?

Citizens vote on local and state laws. But most people do not vote on national laws. Instead, they choose members of Congress to vote for them.

These citizens wait in line to vote.

Members of Congress talk about the bill. They vote to decide if it should be a law. If most members vote for a bill, it goes to the president.

President Barack Obama signs a bill into law.

The president can veto, or reject, a bill. But if the president likes the bill, then he or she signs it. The bill is now a law.

Breaking the Law

Sometimes, people break the law. It can be by accident or on purpose. When people break the law, there are **consequences** (KON-si-kwen-siz).

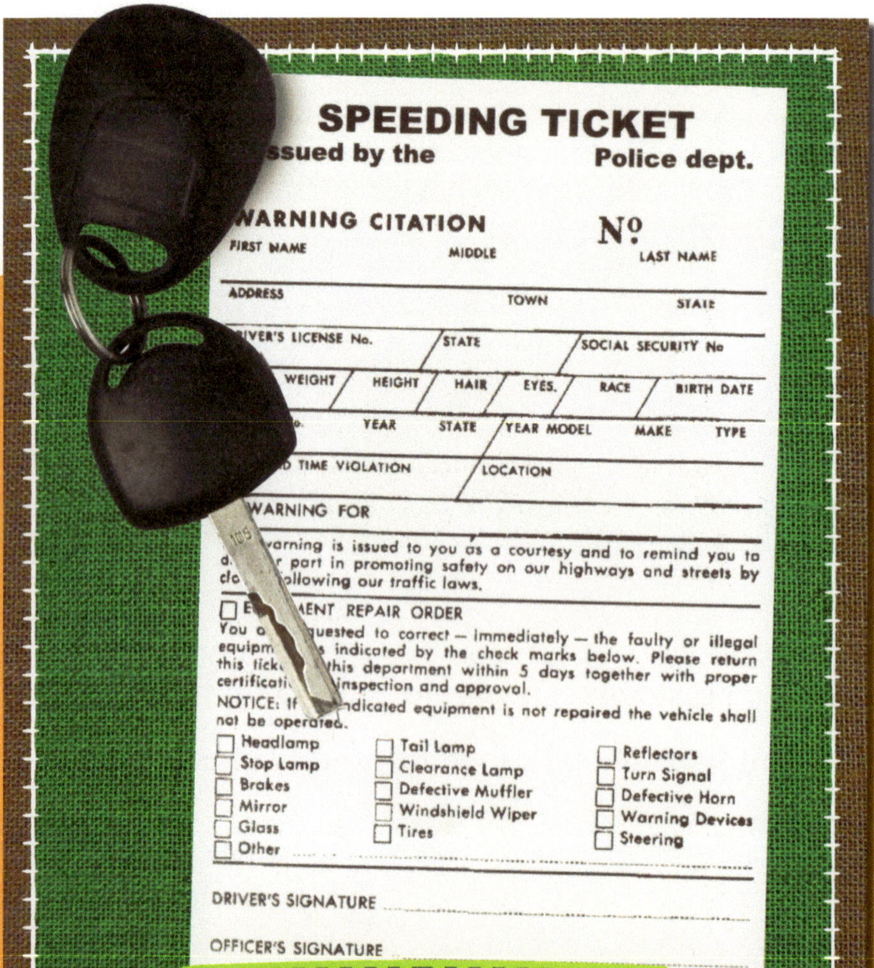

This is a speeding ticket.

There are different types of consequences. A person who drives too fast may get a ticket. If a driver keeps breaking laws, he or she will get in more trouble. The driver might have his or her car taken away.

This car is being taken away.

If a person steals something or hurts someone, he or she may have to go to jail. Spending time in jail is hard.

A police officer takes a person to jail for breaking the law.

When people go to jail, they are not allowed to leave. They have to stay there until their **sentence** is over.

This is a jail cell.

Following the Law

Laws do not work well unless we all follow them. You can be a good citizen by following the law.

Congress

You can help make laws, too. Do you have an idea for a new law? Share your idea with others. It might end up in Congress!

These kids want a law that will stop all wars.

Write It!

Kids must follow the laws, too. What laws do you follow? Make a list.

This girl is listing the laws she follows.

This boy is listing the laws he follows.

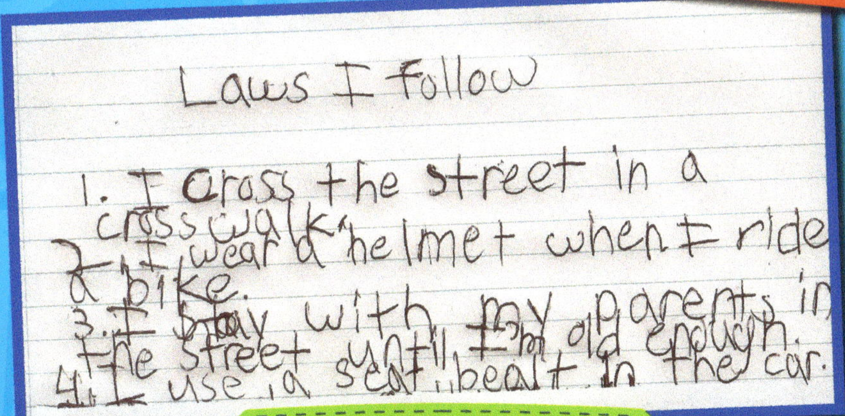

Laws I Follow

1. I cross the street in a crosswalk.
2. I wear a helmet when I ride a bike.
3. I stay with my parents in the street until I'm old enough.
4. I use a seat bealt in the car.

This is the boy's list.

Glossary

amendments—changes in the words or meaning of a law

citizens—members of a country or place

Congress—the group of leaders who make laws for the country

consequences—the results or effects of someone's actions and choices

government—a group of leaders who make choices for a country

laws—rules made by the government

local—relating to a particular area, city, or town

national—relating to an entire nation or country

sentence—the punishment given by a court of law

succeed—to do what you are trying to do

Index

Your Turn!

Our Laws

This photo shows a girl following the law by wearing her seat belt. This law helps keep her safe. If you had to write a new law that would keep people safe, what would it be? Write your law. Share it with your family.